# HAMPSHIRE CRICKET ON THE MOVE

## FROM NORTHLANDS ROAD TO THE ROSE BOWL

RICHARD BINNS

CHIPSTONE BOOKS

First published in 2012 by Chipstone Books
High Trees, Botley Road, Curdridge, Hampshire SO32 2DS
Telephone: 01489 786430

ISBN 978-0-9538204-2-9

Designed by Craig Stevens
www.craig-stevens.co.uk

**To Anne**
Guiding light

## Acknowledgements

I am pleased to acknowledge the many people who helped me in various ways with the preparation of this book and to thank them for so generously offering their time and know-how.

Andrew Milnes, Dave Allen, Jim Marshall, Michael Pain, Mike Barnard, Neil Jenkinson, Nigel Gray, Paul Hendy (Hendy Group Ltd), Philip Bell-Mossley, Richard Pitts, Rod Bransgrove, Simon Vincent, Terry Brewer, Tim Tremlett, Wilfrid Weld and Zac Toumazi.

## Photographs and drawings

Photographs not taken by the author were used with the kind permission of Catherine Binns (p 85), Neil Marshall (pp 70, 94, 96, njmphotographs@yahoo.co.uk), Patrick Eagar (p 86), Getty Images (p 87) Wilfrid Weld (p 17) and Nigel Gray (p 90).

Pictures on pp 36 and 37 came from *Hampshire County Cricket, The Official History* by Altham, Arlott, Eagar and Webber.

I could not trace details of the captains photograph (p 12).

The Shane Warne cartoon (p 19) is by James Husbands (jameshusbands.com).

The sketches throughout the book are by Peter Jarvis (pjarvis.co.uk). Many years ago Helen White did the guide to Northlands Road (p 72) and the late Peter Lucas drew the portraits (p 69).

This book was printed in the UK by Butler Tanner and Dennis, an ISO 14001 accredited company. The printing facility has all operations under one roof and employs mainly local people minimising the energy used in transportation and the manufacturing process. The book was printed using 100% vegetable-based inks on paper which is produced from 100% Elemental Chlorine Free (EFC) pulp that is fully recyclable. It has a Forest Stewardship Council (FSC) accreditation and is produced by a mill which supports well-managed forestry schemes.

# CONTENTS

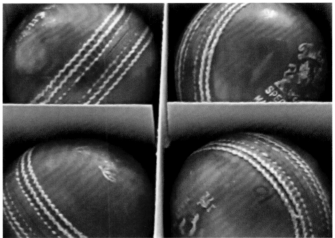

Northlands Road, 12 June, 2000.

# FOREWORD

I was absorbed with Hampshire County Cricket Club at Northlands Road, first as a very young spectator, as a player from 1975 and eventually as Director of Cricket. Now as Cricket Secretary of Hampshire Cricket I am still closely involved with cricketing matters. Across almost fifty years I have seen enormous change, particularly in the last decade.

In the '90s all the facilities at Northlands Road were feeling the strain. For years people had wrestled with the problem that something better was needed and a development site was acquired in 1994.

The move to West End finally happened in 2001. The pavilion was unfinished. Staff worked in Portakabins. During the cricket season coaches, players, physios and umpires used a tented village. Meals were prepared in field kitchens and served under canvas. The bars were in marquees. Even the all-conquering Australians had temporary accommodation, yet they were still gracious when beaten by Hampshire captained by Robin Smith.

From this less than perfect beginning great changes have taken place over the last dozen years. Facilities for players, staff and spectators are second to none. Now the ground is tailored to Test standard. Practice facilities and the Nursery pitch are truly first-class. Our Academy produces a stream of home-grown talent. The golf course on the site is a bonus.

As clearly shown in this book, the journey from Northlands Road to The Rose Bowl produced huge challenges. Remarkable progress has been made under extremely testing conditions. I have been lucky, despite the many storms, to have been involved in that journey. That it is on-going is clear from the very recent re-naming of the ground. Now 'The Ageas Bowl' marks the next stage in the development of Hampshire Cricket.

Tim Tremlett
March 2012

Match day at Northlands Road, 1999.

# INTRODUCTION

Hampshire County Cricket Club's ground at Northlands Road is still talked about with great affection. It was a friendly place, defined to a large extent by the people who had worked there, the characters who watched the matches and all those who had played cricket there for more than a century.

Conveniently close to the centre of Southampton, without doubt it was quaint and full of character. The ground was first used for county matches in the 19th century and still had many facilities built for cricket in that time.

The pictures in this book show the Northlands Road ground at the very end of its days. In the autumn and early winter of the year 2000 it was turned into a building site. I have made 'before and after' comparisons using photographs. These illustrate the last weeks of the old cricket ground and also show its subsequent development as a site for town houses.

Since the start of the millennium, Hampshire's out-of town ground has been made into an outstanding cricket venue: purpose-built, ultra-modern in design and now an established choice for international fixtures.

At the end of the book some final reminders of Northlands Road show a clear but, I hope, sympathetic contrast with The Rose Bowl, the new home of Hampshire Cricket.

City End scoreboard.

# CLEARING THE DECKS

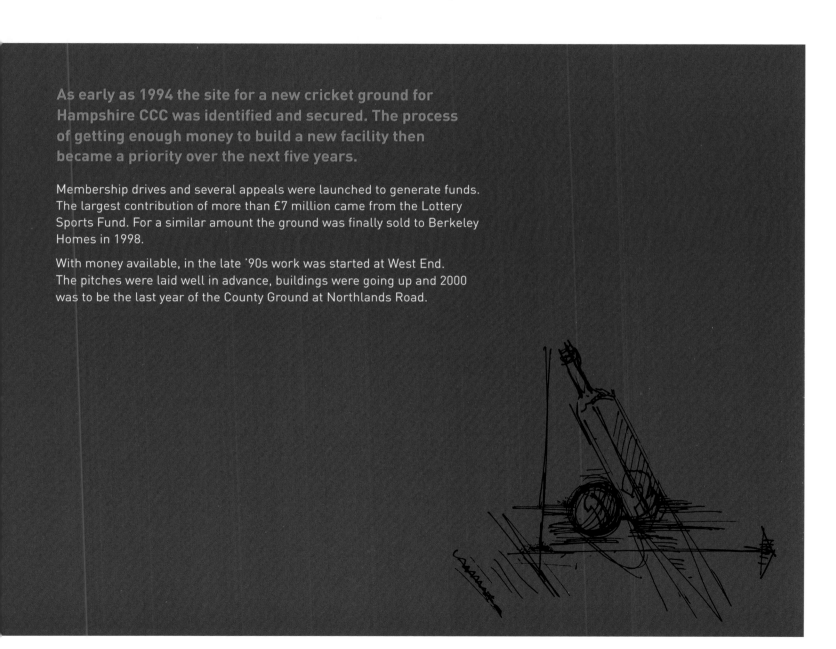

As early as 1994 the site for a new cricket ground for Hampshire CCC was identified and secured. The process of getting enough money to build a new facility then became a priority over the next five years.

Membership drives and several appeals were launched to generate funds. The largest contribution of more than £7 million came from the Lottery Sports Fund. For a similar amount the ground was finally sold to Berkeley Homes in 1998.

With money available, in the late '90s work was started at West End. The pitches were laid well in advance, buildings were going up and 2000 was to be the last year of the County Ground at Northlands Road.

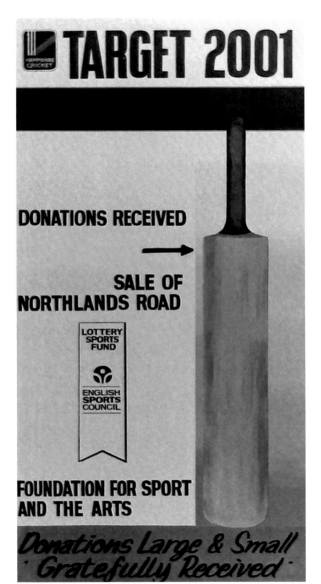

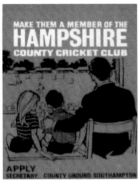

Various fund raising appeals were launched.

▲ The 'Sponsor a Tree' poster gave a sketch preview of the new ground.

➤ In 1996, scoreboard numbers make up the figure awarded by the Lottery Fund for the development of the new ground.

The players are John Stephenson, Kevin James, Jim Bovill, Shaun Udal, Adie Ames, Robin Smith and Derek Kenway.

▼ The last game was played to a full house. At the end of that day many spectators stayed on at the ground a little longer than usual. People scrambled for the souvenirs which the players threw to the crowd. For the following week a Farewell Dinner was being arranged to mark the end of an era of first-class cricket in Southampton.

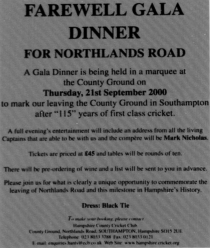

The dinner had been a sell-out and was a great success.

◀ The morning after the night before.

Guests included a line-up of Hampshire worthies who had captained the county team between 1958 and 2000.

Richard Gilliat, Robin Smith, John Stephenson, Mark Nicholas, Nick Pocock, Bob Stephenson and Colin Ingleby-Mackenzie.

The marquees from the dinner were still on the ground the following morning but the job of clearing the site was already well under way.

In front of the pavilion where members had just a few days before spilled out from the bar to watch the game there were now empty terraces.

People used to enjoy being able to watch the players practise in the nets, which were close to the main entrance.

In his England kit, Angus Fraser loosens up before the game.

Part of the clearance process involved raising as much money as possible from the sale of almost everything in the ground which was movable. This gave members of the public a final chance to get a souvenir of the old ground.

One Saturday morning the buyers came and the nets area was filled with memorabilia of all kinds: the physio table, parts of the scoreboard, an office sign, pavilion tables, souvenirs of the bar.

As a result of the sale, mementos of the ground are scattered around the south of England. Sections of balustrade from the Ladies' Pavilion enhance a border.

A sign saved from the bonfire now hangs in a cluttered garage.

◄ Once built into the Northlands Road perimeter wall, the turnstile kiosk was rescued and restored.

▼ The stained glass panel, just visible in the photo behind ex-players Mike Taylor and Andy Murtagh, is a last remnant of the Philip Mead Stand.

More significant pieces of club memorabilia were collected and kept by the Heritage Group.
Some of these have been used to decorate parts of the new pavilion at The Rose Bowl.
One of the most treasured is the clock in the Shackleton Bar.

Presented by Brylcreem, the clock was made by Tucker, Munn and Grimshaw Ltd,
24 Rhodesia House, Hatton Gardens, London.

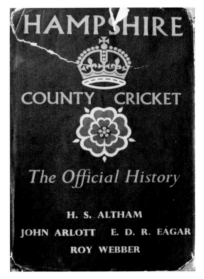

Shane Warne played in the last match at Northlands Road and signed the ball used in that game (17 September 2000).

Still going strong, Terry Brewer signals the start of play from the balcony of The Rose Bowl pavilion.

The 'Athlone Castle' bell is, for many, a regular reminder of cricket at Northlands Road.

Mechanical jaws tear down the pavilion, 10 October, 2000.

# DEMOLITION IN PROGRESS

**Demolition started in earnest soon after the Farewell Dinner and by October 2000 work was well under way.**

The terracing was limited, most of the pavilion structure was wood and the Philip Mead Stand was designed as semi-permanent accommodation for spectators.

For the wrecking crew and their machines this presented no problems. Within a couple of weeks it was all over.

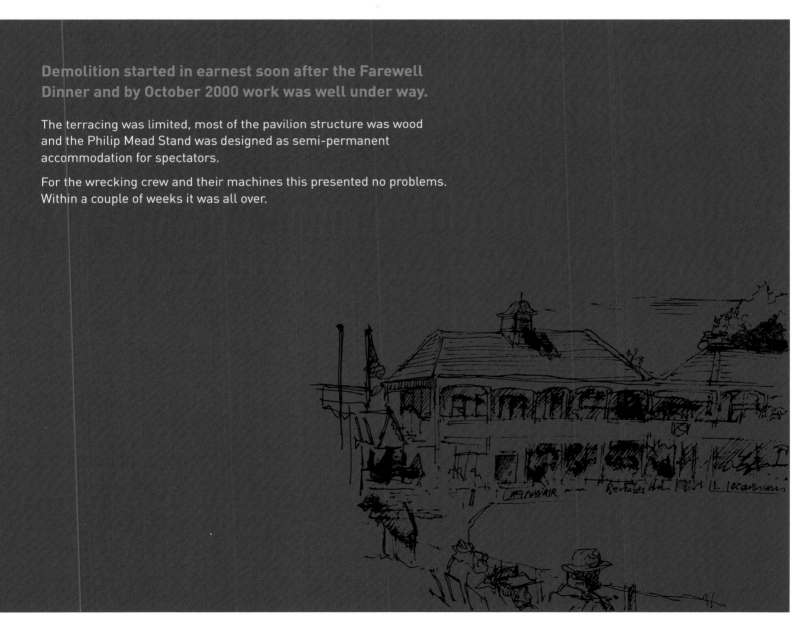

The first section of the ground to go was the terracing alongside the pavilion.

▲ John Stephenson bowling from the Northlands Road End.

The half dozen rows of seats mounted on planks fixed to scaffolding frames were no match for the machines.

Still standing is the cubicle from which volunteers broadcast match commentaries on the local hospital radio system.

For many years Berkeley Homes was prominently advertised around the ground.

The company eventually bought the land for development and flew the company flag when demolition began.

The pavilion had been so elegant for many summers. Now it was roughly shaken like an empty box as the mechanical digger began to tear it to pieces.

Tiles flew, beams tumbled and the east end of the pavilion was wrecked within minutes.

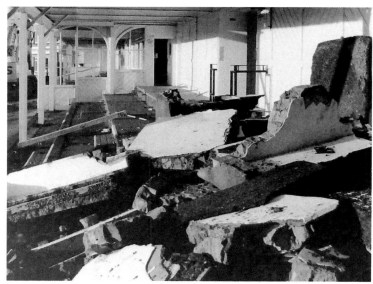

Contrasting photos show the view across to the flats on the east side of the ground.

The seating under the pavilion and in the rest of the ground was packed to capacity in mid-summer 1999.

Just over a year later the scene was one of empty terracing and of rubble.

With the demolition of the pavilion almost complete, the landmark cupola was carefully taken from the roof. It has a top cover and side flashings of lead and large structural timbers so a hefty crane was needed for lifting. Close-up it is surprisingly large.

➤ The cupola is now safely stored. Hopefully, it could one day be seen again as a feature at The Ageas Bowl.

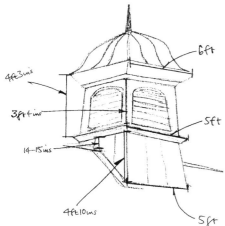

# PAVILION HISTORY

1887

1895

On 9 May 1885 the inaugural event at the ground was a grand bazaar.

The first county cricket match was played at Northlands Road a week later.

Between 1887 and 1895 twin structures were built on each side of the original pavilion.

1895

1999

Compare the 1895 picture with a later modern photo of the pavilion.

The spacing of the windows and the doors on the ground floor suggests that the base of the original single storey building was the template for later expansion of the pavilion.

**1951**

The re-modelled pavilion was duplicated to provide a Ladies' Pavilion.

**1999**

The two pavilions were eventually connected in 1964.

More than any other feature on the ground, the building used by the Hampshire players as a dressing room encapsulated the essence of Northlands Road.

True, it was picturesque. At the same time, it was too small for the job and had barely adequate facilities.

Despite this, it was an important focal point. It was squashed between the pavilion and the main admin block. Close behind it were the groundsman's house and offices for the support services.

By accident rather than by design, on match days it brought the players, the umpires, other officials, spectators and autograph collectors within touching distance of each other.

It was this closeness of all the participants at the game which gave the ground an atmosphere which was unique.

Members get to their seats as Hampshire's opponents come out to field.

Umpires Palmer and Clarkson are ready to start the day's play.

West Indies batsman Keith Arthurton signs autographs under the balcony.

Members had seats practically under the changing room balcony. For many spectators, being so close to the action was a big attraction. The players also felt a rapport with the members standing to greet them as they came down the steps on to the outfield.

Leading Hampshire out to field, Robin Smith is followed by Adie Aymes, Peter Hartley and Matthew Keech.

Physio Dave Newman, Terry Brewer, Tim Tremlett and Alex Morris relax on the balcony.

Below them a steward controls the entrance to the members' seating in front of the pavilion.

➤ Clear signage points the way to the ancient, rather basic but vital facilities just round the corner.

To start the day the umpires turned right from their little room behind the players' pavilion, passed the physio's door and walked down an alleyway. Through the narrowing in single file and going under the balcony of the changing room they finally emerged into the sunlight and on to the pitch.

The skeleton-like fencing traces that same pathway.

The players' changing room was built more than a century before this photo was taken. Immediately recognizable, it was the oldest original building on the Northlands Road ground. With the main pavilion already flattened it was a forlorn sight , soon destined for the skip.

Lying on the ground are the windows from the Philip Mead Stand.

The stand was named after Hampshire's all-time top run scorer. Mead had an astonishing career record of 48,892 runs in 701 matches, 138 centuries and an average of 48.84.

The painter's view of the pavilion disappeared.

The balconies of the flats which ran down the length of the east side of the ground provided a grandstand view of the cricket.

On the other hand, they were within reasonably easy reach of a ball hit out of the meat of the bat.

There is a story of an occupant who had been bombarded so many times that one day, in protest, he held up a match for a while by refusing to return the ball which had just come through his lounge window.

Against the background of the flats, Alex Tudor of Surrey and England patiently signs for the autograph collectors.

The end of an innings. Raj Maru leaves the field followed by the Glamorgan team.

After the toss Brian Lara and Stephen Fleming go back to their teams. The West Indies batted first in a World Cup game against New Zealand.

For spectators the outfield was a meeting place, for children a playing field and for the autograph hunters a fruitful collecting area.

The ground had been carefully tended for more than a hundred years.

The quality of the square and the outfield was appreciated by the Hampshire players, their county visitors and established internationals alike.

The 'everything must go' sale made the local evening news. Turf was sold by the yard.

➤ Finally, the whole site was reduced to mud, bricks and puddles.

Commemorative plaque, Marshall Square.

This plaque marks
The site of
The County Cricket Ground
Home of Hampshire County Cricket Club
1885 - 2000

# NORTHLANDS ROAD THEN AND NOW

**Cricket was first played by the Hampshire County Cricket Club (HCCC) at The Antelope Ground in Southampton. This was in Saint Mary's Road and was opposite the hotel from which the ground took its name. At that time the cost of annual membership of the Club was fixed at one guinea (£1.05).**

After ten years at The Antelope, in 1885 a flourishing HCCC moved to The County Ground for which the Club paid an annual rental of £160. Incidentally, soon after Southampton Football Club also moved from Saint Mary's and became established close by at The Dell. The two grounds were only a few hundred yards apart and Northlands Road, which was eventually synonymous with The County Ground, became a main route to matches for both cricket and football supporters.

A separate company, The Hampshire County Ground Company, was formed in 1893. Its aim was to buy the freehold of the land and also to raise sufficient funds for buildings. This was done successfully by inviting the public to purchase shares in the company. (A similar scheme was to be re-run by Rose Bowl plc many years later after the move from Northlands Road to the West End stadium).

Eventually the growth and spread of Southampton overtook and overwhelmed both Northlands Road and The Dell. They became surrounded by housing. The load which modern transport would impose on them and the standards later required by their faithful supporters became too much. Inevitably both had to re-locate. This relocation of HCCC to a third home ground was another step in its growth.

Northlands Road is slowly becoming history. Even now the images grow less distinct and memory fades. However, a permanent reminder of the past is given by the street names which survive. Charles Knott Gardens, Arlott Court, Greenidge Court and Marshall Square will always tell of the time when people in their thousands used to come to watch professional cricket played in this quiet city suburb.

1999

2011

The tree remains as a marker (seen also on p 49).

A plaque marks the entrance to Marshall Square where the old gates into the ground used to be.

The large block facing the road is where the pavilion stood.

Gates and turnstiles have been replaced by a wall,
fencing and a decorative hedge.

The area in front of the groundsman's cottage is still a car park. The sign now reads 'Residents Only'.

The tree to the left of the picture was by the main entrance.

◄ Flagseller on the day the West Indies came to town.

This tree has grown. No match day excitement in Edwin Jones Green and Arlott Court these days.

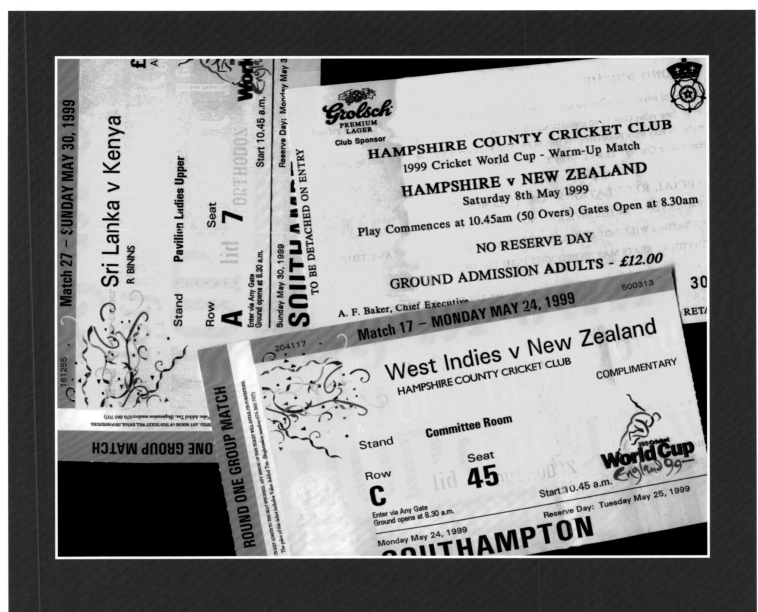

The near corner of the block of apartments is roughly where the admin offices, the players' changing room and the west end of the main pavilion stood.

➤ The wall and the seating running down to the trees on the far right have been replaced by a terrace of houses. The boundary at the Northlands Road End is now a road to more housing.

The flats overlooked the spectators by the boundary wall. Now the view
from the balconies is of parking spaces behind a terrace of houses.

The east side of the ground towards the City End.

➤ The green refuse bins are on the spot where deep backward square leg was fielding with Brian Lara batting in 1999.

The former nets area is now an ornamental garden.

Parts of the development are named after three Hampshire greats:
Gordon Greenidge, Roy Marshall and Malcolm Marshall.

➤ Imposing entrance to Greenidge Court.

Jimmy Adams. Hampshire v Nottinghamshire, 8 June 2006.

# HAMPSHIRE CRICKET AT THE ROSE BOWL

Many years before the County Ground was demolished, it was clear that cricket in Hampshire did need a new, out-of-town location. Even in the '80s and early '90s this idea had already begun to move gradually towards reality. The site for a ground was acquired in 1994. Initial funds had been obtained and in 1997 the project got under way with the start of massive ground works which shaped the site at West End.

If those first involved and responsible for the initial planning of Hampshire's new ground had been asked at the very earliest stages to look into the future, it now seems unlikely that they could have imagined how massive the task of building The Rose Bowl would eventually become or just how breathtaking the outcome would be.

Not wishing to end on a doleful note, I have used this last section to give a final reminder of the old County Ground but also to show something of its spectacular replacement, The Rose Bowl.

The story of the development of The Rose Bowl is still unfolding. It has become a long, complex and intriguing one which warrants separate illustration sometime in the future.

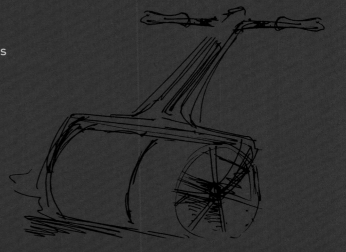

The surrounding maze of streets often made parking difficult but the old ground was just a short distance from public transport available in central Southampton.

Easily accessible, The Rose Bowl is close to the motorway network. Large car parks are available on site. Park and ride service and buses from local train stations are provided on big match days.

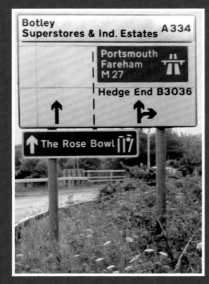

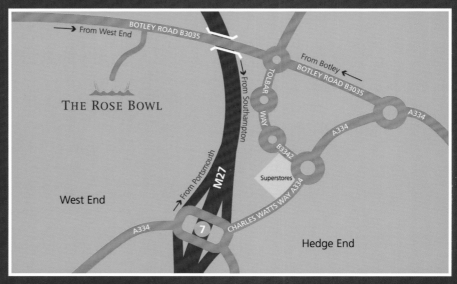

NORTHLANDS ROAD

1999

Going to the cricket.

2011

Perhaps after walking from Southampton's railway station or parking in surrounding streets, spectators come down Northlands Road towards the main gate into the ground.

⋏ To get to the West Gate entrance spectators cross the tree-lined road from one of the large parking areas.

➤ Steps down from the road lead to the bank of turnstiles close to the imposing West Stand.

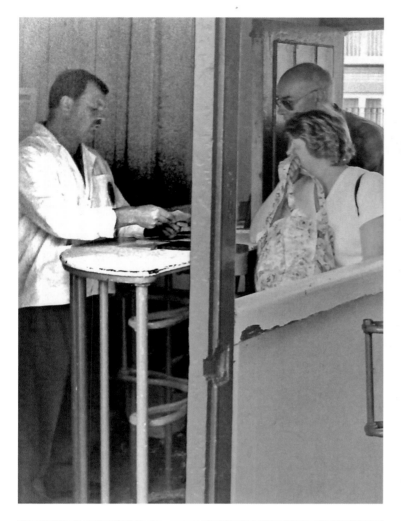

Each of the three mechanised entrances to the old ground had two turnstiles.

At the turnstile an attendant collected the entrance money or tickets, operated a simple foot pedal, the supporter gave a shove and joined the crowd.

The bank of modern turnstiles at the West Gate allows automated entry to the ground.

Barcodes on pre-paid tickets or data on membership cards are read, entry details logged and the turnstile unlocks.

As at the fast lane in the supermarket, a kind assistant is available to guide those not familiar with the check-in procedure.

Seating at the City End of the ground at Northlands Road.

In 1999, avid Hampshire supporters Terry Webb, David Hutchinson and Mick Bowring enjoy the game from the bench under the balcony of the players' changing room at Northlands Road.

The roof towers over the spectators packed into the 2000-seater capacity West Stand at The Rose Bowl.

Twelve years on, and by a complete coincidence, this photo shows Terry and Mick watching a 2nd team game at the Nursery Ground. For some reason, David couldn't come out to play that day.

▲ A busy day in the members' bar and the upstairs dining room at Northlands Road.

◀ Members' facilities in The Rose Bowl pavilion.

The spacious Atrium is a reception area and lounge which links the main pavilion to the indoor cricket school, conference rooms and staff offices.

With food freshly prepared in on-site kitchens and with a view across the ground, diners in the Shackleton Bar enjoy the lunch interval.

⊼ From 1997 Nigel Gray, while still working at the old County Ground, was closely involved at the new site with the planning and development of the main cricket ground, the nursery pitch and the golf course. His knowledge and experience at Northlands Road were key to the preparation of top class playing surfaces from the starting point of a rough field by the motorway.

⊻ Still working on the ground at The Rose Bowl, Mark Miller and Dave Henbrey also brought years of experience from Northlands Road.

 Using the most up-to-date turf management techniques and equipment, the groundstaff have worked hard on the playing surface in fair weather and foul.

Innovations such as automatic watering and excellent drainage systems were installed when the new ground was laid. After a bedding down period, the relatively new square has settled, the outfield is like a carpet and The Rose Bowl is now a Test venue.

◀ Always hands-on, Nigel Gray talks to Jimmy Adams during a rain break and works on re-laying and re-seeding wickets at the end of the season.

Pictures at Northlands Road showing both ends
of the cricket ground.

➤ Basically the same subjects but quite different views for the
two ladies at The Rose Bowl, with a computerised scoreboard,
floodlights, the tented roof of the pavilion and imposing stands.

Hampshire v Scotland one-day game at The Rose Bowl, 4 August 2003.

All whites, cable-knit sweaters, white flannel shirts and pants and blanco-ed leather boots. Richard Gilliat's team enjoys, with quiet satisfaction, a season's effort to win the County Championship trophy in 1973.

Little did the '73 team know that cricket was on the verge of enormous change over the next three decades.

Now we have a two division Championship with promotion and relegation, helmets, white balls, coloured kit, sponsorship, floodlit cricket, Twenty20, power plays, third umpires, umpire decision review system, covered wickets, Hawk Eye, hot spots, Snickometer, fitness coaches, beep tests, sunglasses as head gear, technologically advanced fabrics, Duckworth-Lewis, Kolpak players, corridors of uncertainty.

In 2005 a more roisterous celebration by the winners of the one-day Cheltenham and Gloucester Trophy.

**Hampshire**
Cricket

**Hampshire**
Royals

Iron brackets supporting the balcony of the old pavilion.

The graceful curve of one of the award-winning stands* at The Rose Bowl.

*Structural Steel Design Awards, 2011

The cupola provided ventilation of the roof space and shelter for the birds.

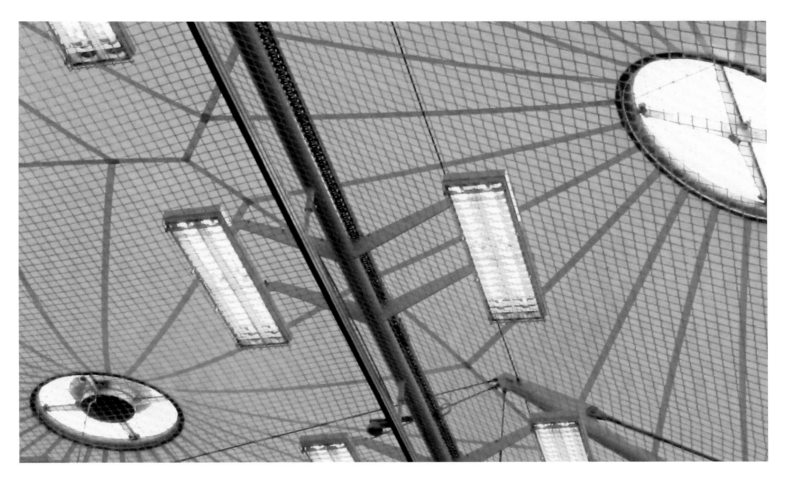

➤ Skylights in the roof of the indoor nets.

◄ Cleaning the roof of the cricket school.

1999

2011

Inaugural Test match at The Rose Bowl, June 2011.

# POSTSCRIPT

**We are about to start the twelfth season at Hampshire Cricket's new out-of-town ground. The development of the ground has been a long process, from the phase of first landscaping a rough piece of farmland to the staged building of an ultra-modern cricket facility.**

Perversely, it was the construction of this stadium which was to threaten the very existence of first-class cricket in Hampshire. During the earliest stage of work an extensive search for additional financial support and, in particular, a Naming Rights sponsor had been unsuccessful. The ambitious project exceeded initial budgets and proved to be beyond the financial capabilities of Hampshire County Cricket Club.

It was against this backdrop that Rose Bowl plc took Hampshire Cricket into private ownership in 2001 and began the process of building a sustainable business around it. In the short-term this involved encouraging international and Test match cricket to The Rose Bowl and this, in itself, required further and significant funding.

Although at a very high standard now, this magnificent stadium remains work in progress and the business plans of Rose Bowl plc remain uncompleted. However, in February 2012, we were able to announce a very special partnership with local insurance company Ageas which resulted in renaming The Rose Bowl to The Ageas Bowl. The liaison provides us with a local partner of real size and substance and with values which match our own. In our pursuit of long-term stability for Hampshire Cricket, we believe that this relationship will be critical and that the circa 150-year history of this great club will be enhanced and consolidated at The Ageas Bowl.

I look forward with optimism to the next chapter in this fascinating story.

Rod Bransgrove
March 2012